C000101476

Extinct

April De Angelis's plays include *Rune* (Stoke Theatre), *My Brilliant Friend* (adapted from Elena Ferrante's novels for Rose Theatre, Kingston, and NT), *House Party* (BBC4 and Headlong Theatre), *Gin Craze!*, a musical with Lucy Rivers (Royal & Derngate), *The Village* (Stratford East),*Wild East* (Royal Court), *A Laughing Matter* (Out of Joint/NT/tour), *The Warwickshire Testimony* (RSC), *The Positive Hour* (Out of Joint/Hampstead/Old Vic; Sphinx), *Headstrong* (NT Shell Connections), *Playhouse Creatures* (Sphinx Theatre Company), *Hush* (Royal Court), *Soft Vengeance* (Graeae Theatre Company), *The Life and Times of Fanny Hill* (adapted from the James Cleland novel), *Ironmistress* (ReSisters Theatre Company), *Wuthering Heights* (adapted from Emily Brontë's novel for Birmingham Rep), *Jumpy* (Royal Court and Duke of York's Theatres), *Gastronauts* (Royal Court), and *After Electra* (Theatre Royal, Plymouth). Her work for BBC Radio includes *Visitants*, *The Outlander*, which won the Writers' Guild Award 1992, and *Cash Cows* for the *Woman's Hour* serial. For opera: *Flight* with composer Jonathan Dove (Glyndebourne), and the libretto for *Silent Twins* (Almeida).

APRIL DE ANGELIS

Extinct

faber

First published in 2021
by Faber and Faber Limited
74–77 Great Russell Street
London WC1B 3DA

Typeset by Brighton Gray
Printed and bound in the UK by CPI Group (Ltd), Croydon CR0 4YY

A CIP record for this book
is available from the British Library

978-0-571-37388-8

2 4 6 8 10 9 7 5 3 1

STRATFORD EAST

A printing error led to a mistake in billing,
please see amended creative team details below:

April Kiran Landa

Director and Dramaturg Kirsty Housley
Designer Peter McKintosh
Lighting Designer Joshua Pharo
Sound Designer Melanie Wilson
Video Designer Nina Dunn
Assistant Director Germma Orleans-Thompson
Design Associate Alice Hallifax
Associate Sound Designer Tingying Dong
Video Design Associate Libby Ward

Extinct was first performed at Theatre Royal Stratford East, London, on 30 June 2021, with the following cast and creative team:

April Kiran Landa

Director Kirsty Housley
Designer Peter McKintosh
Lighting Designer Joshua Pharo
Sound Designer Melanie Wilson
Video Designer Nina Dunn
Assistant Director Gemma Orleans-Thompson
Design Associate Alice Hallifax
Associate Sound Designer Tingying Dong
Video Design Associate Libby Ward

Characters

April

Suhayla and **Abani**
*start out as recorded voices
but are taken over by the actor*

Plus the recorded voices of

Helen Burnett
Rob Callender
Sue Hampton
Kay Michaels
Chidi Obihara
Lola Perrin
Leslie Tate
Aaron Thierry
Xanthe
Elise Yarde

*This text went to press during rehearsals and may differ in
performance.*

EXTINCT

CAPTION: *The Anthropocene; the age of human-made climate change.*

1. FUTURE NIGHTMARE

April I want you to imagine me in a crowd of people. The year is 2030 and the mean temperature this summer has been forty degrees Celsius. It's midday. The sun is nuclear hot. There have been spontaneous outbreaks of fires round the country, the closest to us in Epping Forest, a monster conflagration which raged for three weeks. The air still tastes of ash.

It was this year the three breadbaskets of the world in the USA, Central Russia and South East Asia failed due to high temperatures, drought and fire leading to a catastrophic global shortage of carbohydrates. Added to that, unseasonal rainfall here meant that the potato crop which might have compensated rotted in the ground – it was the first time the UK had been subject to rationing since World War II.

And there was panic. Supermarkets stripped bare. Looting began – people convinced that stores of food were being kept from them – nights of smashed windows and marauding gangs. Then onto the streets came the army. There was a shoot-out at Westfield's in the Marks and Spencer's food hall. The government stepped in with a new plan. Since then a fragile peace has descended. Food distribution depots were designated, one member of each household could be dispatched plus ration card to pick up a bag of pasta or flour, a few tins, perhaps some dried pulses. A fortnight's supply. All anyone talks about is food.

People will kill for a sachet of yeast.

I came on my bike which I locked up safely several streets away. Now in the crowd, as anxiety and hunger pricks us, the emotion turns sour. Near me a fight breaks out. People turn on the one who they say was pushing in. The guy is near tears – his kids are hungry, his wife is sick. It turns mean. The thud of fists on flesh. I try to raise my voice but no one hears me. The press of bodies is claustrophobic. Ahead, the iron shutter at the depot is drawn down halfway and a woman appears.

Why have they chosen a woman? Do they think we will forgive her more easily? She asks the crowd to disperse. *The depot is now empty. We will reopen tomorrow at 8 a.m. when another delivery is expected.* They can only provide for the last twenty queuers. People mutter. They know they are being fobbed off. The armed security guards at her side look on impassively though I can imagine sweat pricking their armpits. Someone once told me that in cities we are only ever six meals away from starvation but I had dismissed it. I lived a short walk away from twenty fast-food outlets. What about Deliveroo?

Something like a moan rises from the crowd. The unbearable thought of another hungry night, the faces of their disappointed, bewildered kids, their cries of hunger.

There is a sudden jolt forwards. I am caught in a vast river of bodies. Part of me wants to run back to my bike, flee the madness, but another part is thinking – I've stood here for two hours in punishing sun and now to be told to return home with nothing? I too taste anger, bitterness. How has this been allowed to happen? We were not born to go hungry. I'm too far back from the front and I feel guilty – I had stopped off on the way by the canal – there was a lone duck meandering along the puddling water. I wanted the

normal so badly as I waited there transfixed to the spot.
Wishing myself back
 A year, two years, five, a decade – to when there was still
time to do something about it.

At the front someone has pulled the woman from her
platform into the crowd, she vanishes like a stone into a
pond and the first shot is fired.

*Lighting changes. The woman is standing alone. We can
now see the whole space. She looks at us.*

Hello.
 Thanks for coming.
 I have an hour to convert you to the cause of climate
change
 So we can avoid the kind of nightmare I just imagined.
 So we can change our future.

We live on a finely balanced, beautifully temperate Earth
that has sustained human life for two hundred thousand
years, But all that, unfortunately, is changing.

As a playwright I ask myself what's the point of me, of
theatre, in a time of crisis, if I'm not raising the alarm so
that we can avoid unnecessary suffering?

Aristotle's advice to playwrights was: 'Don't make your
story so small that it can be consumed in one bite, or too
big, like an animal so huge you can't take in both its head
and its tail.' Climate change is just like that – a hyperobject
– a conceptual fact so large, so complex, like the internet, it
can never be properly comprehended.

So I have my work cut out for me.

I'm standing here talking to you
 Coming across as quite a rational calm individual
 But don't be fooled. Inside I'm screaming.
 I'm panicking.

5

I can see the waters rising over our heads
And I'm shouting, It's the end of the world
But no one can hear me.

Sorry.

There have been five previous mass extinctions.

The most lethal was two hundred and fifty million years ago when volcanic eruptions released enough carbon dioxide to warm the oceans by ten degrees Celsius ending ninety-six per cent of marine life and seventy per cent of life on Earth. The event known as the Great Dying.

We are now experiencing the sixth mass extinction.

Humans are emitting greenhouse gases ten times faster than the volcanoes did during the Great Dying.

There is no single peer-reviewed paper
    Published in the last twenty-five years that would contradict this scenario
    Every living system of Earth is in decline
    Every life support system of Earth is in decline.

I'm feeling that thing where it feels impossible
    Breaking into a sweat
    It's supposed to be that telling people helps to control the anxiety every time I do this I have to go into it again
    It's not a place I like to go.
    I have to be calm though – no one wants to hear someone shouting at them hysterically, being emotional. Getting naked and covering myself in crude oil is not going to help my cause.
    Still, I want to explain as calmly as I can the shit we're in.

If I feel really anxious I tend to snack – so I'm just going to do that now.

Takes out a sweet – eats it. Then is left with the wrapper. Holds up the wrapper.

Is there somewhere I can put this?
Somewhere I can throw it away?

She looks.

I'll come clean. This was planned.
This – what is it – a prop? – it was something in the real
world
Now it's kind of standing in for itself
Just like I'm an actor standing in for the writer.

It was something until it became the opposite – nothing.
Something to be forgotten.
Is it recyclable?

She drops it in a bin.

There, forgotten – vanished – someone else's problem
We like to imagine we can throw things away with no
consequence.
But we've made 'away' up
Away is somewhere we have been encouraged not to see
Away is our future
And if we don't act until we feel the climate crisis is upon
us, we will all beommitted to solving a problem that can no
longer be solved.

So in 2018 I went to a meeting of a new group called
Extinction Rebellion in the old Limehouse library.
They were concerned about the government's inaction on
the climate and ecological emergency.
That we were being kept in the dark.

I expected to find six people and a dog.
I walked into the biggest meeting I had ever attended in
my life
We got into smaller groups and went round sharing why
we were here
In my group were two local schoolgirls.
One, said I'm here because when I die because of climate
change I want to know I tried to do something about it.

The advice everyone gave me was educate yourself. I wanted to know everything.

I did a lot of research.

She gestures to screen.

CAPTIONS:
   '*The Uninhabitable Earth*' David Wallace-Wells
   '*How to Talk About Climate Change in a Way That Makes a Difference*' Rebecca Huntley
   '*This Changes Everything*' Naomi Klein
   '*On Fire*' Naomi Klein
   '*The Future We Choose*' Christiana Figueres
   '*Falter*' Bill McKibben
   '*Boiling Point*' Bill McKibben
   '*This Is Not A Drill: An Extinction Rebellion Handbook*'
   '*The Great Derangement*' Amitav Ghosh
   '*Corona, Climate, Chronic Emergency*' Andreas Malm
   '*The Climate Majority*' Leo Barasi
   '*Our House is On Fire*' GretaThunberg and Malena Ernman
   '*We Are the Weather*' Jonathan Safran Foer

A little light reading there.

Here's a quote from *This Is Not A Drill*
   The Extinction Rebellion Handbook
   It's got a lovely pink cover and the comforting penguin icon but don't let that fool you – it's a dead penguin.

'This is our darkest hour; Humanity finds itself embroiled in an event unprecedented in its history, one which unless immediately addressed will catapult us further into the destruction of all we hold dear; this nation, its peoples, our ecosystems and the future generations to come.'

Or as David Wallace-Wells says, 'It's worse, much worse than you think.'

Naomi Klein says our lives will change.
    The choice is whether we are going to be in control of
that change
    Or it's going to happen to us in the most terrifying way.

I talked to a lot of activists.

Kay (*voice-over*) I read *This Changes Everything*
    I bloody love Naomi Klein
    I nosedived into it all
    A real light-bulb moment for me – an undeniable need
for a massive change in everything.

Chidi (*voice-over*) What's more important than your right
and ability to breathe?
    What's more important than having good-quality food to
eat
    And clean water to drink?

Lola (*voice-over*) I stayed in my bedroom for six weeks
    That was grief and I literally did not know what to do
    With the heat beating down and knowing people were
dying from the heat all over Europe.

Elise (*voice-over*) I remember walking into my first non-
violent direct-action training
    And the first thing that popped into my head was like,
where are all the people of colour?
    I was actually like, confused by it – like this is
Walthamstow, there are brown people everywhere!

Xanthe (*voice-over*) A lot of my friends don't really
understand that like, yeah, I live in a field. But they're still
supportive, I'm still friends with them.

Rob (*voice-over*) I remember just from school – I'd been to
the Amazon, a lucky kid, and found out that one of the
places I'd been to no longer exists.
    And things like that really made me begin to think
obsessively.

Aaron (*voice-over*) One of the things is, collectively sharing our emotions in public

   Is a healthy thing to do but it also gives us the language and sense of community we need in order to face up to the realities

   Shared – collective grieving.

Chidi (*voice-over*) During COP26 we need to try and convince all one hundred and twenty-six members to stop financing new fossil fuel projects. We have to draw a line in the sand in 2021, we need to stop growing an industry that harms us all physically, economically, biologically, socially. We need to persuade them to keep it in the ground.

Sue (*voice-over*) I volunteered to be an oil-slick rebel, perfect for me cos I don't really feel that I can do something that's very obviously arrestable.

   PROJECTION: *Image of oil-slick rebel.*

Helen (*voice-over*) I was arrested on the first day trying to get the ARC onto the bridge – a great symbol

   I felt incredibly peaceful when they arrested me. I was in a very prayerful place.

April Before we start, this show comes with a warning
   The storyteller's pact
   Come with me
   We'll go places, sure
   But I'll bring you safely back
   Home
   To dry land
   This story is different
   I apologise
   In advance
   I can't tell it
   With that same certainly.

   CAPTION: *Air.*

The last decade was the warmest ever recorded in the UK. In the summer of 2019 temperatures reached thirty-eight-point-five degrees. Trains were evacuated because of melting overhead cables. Our government's committee on climate change warned we are not prepared for the increase in heatwaves that will come with global warming.

There is now more CO_2 in our atmosphere than at any other time in recorded history – in 2019 humans released forty-three billion tons of it.

Lola (*voice-over*) Like what did CO_2 do?
    Someone said, Imagine an orange that you never take the peel off
    And I began to visualise it through that
    It's the peel, the CO_2 released by the burning of fossil fuels, that traps all the heat in.
    Cooks the orange.

April Methane, another greenhouse gas, is also emitted from the burning of fossil fuels, from livestock and farming. Per unit, it is eighty-five times stronger than CO_2 and the second biggest contributor to global heating. In 2020 methane had hit the highest levels ever on record.

These particles which trap heat from the sun are also lethal to breathe. *Globally, ten thousand people daily are dying from air pollution.*

We tend to trivialise the differences between the heating of degrees above pre-industrial levels, one point five, two or four, because these numbers seem so small – but at two degrees, four hundred million more people will suffer from water scarcity. At three degrees, Southern Europe would be in permanent drought. At four degrees, there would be annual global food crises, the Alps would be as arid as the Atlas Mountains
    And if we hit eight degrees

A third of the planet would be made unlivable by direct heat.

At these temperatures the human body can't expel heat and basically cooks.

But we won't need to get to eight degrees
to be in serious shit.

Leslie (*voice-over*) It's a terrible experience to realise what's going to happen which, you know, yeah we're doing our best to stop it but we can wipe ourselves out

And our children, our grandchildren, are going to go through terrible experiences.

These temperatures are averages, some places are rising much faster than others.

Aaron (*voice-over*) The Arctic is warming maybe three times as fast of the rest of the planet because you get this amplification process.

April Hot air melts the white ice in the Arctic which then stops reflecting the sun's rays back out into space, and the shiny white mirror is replaced with dull blue seawater which instead absorbs the sun's heat and then the warmer sea shrinks yet more ice. It's called the Albedo effect.

This is an example of a feedback loop.

Hidden ice locked beneath the soils of the Arctic is now starting to melt fast too, and as that permafrost thaws, microbes convert some of that frozen material into methane and carbon dioxide which is released and causes yet more warming –

Incidentally that's not all that could be released – microbes like the bubonic plague and the Spanish flu are lurking in the ancient melting ice – what new pandemics might be unleashed?

As our atmosphere heats, warm air holds more water vapour than cold, providing additional fuel for storms and hurricanes. In addition, sea level rise increases the amount of sea water that is pushed onto shore during coastal storms. In 2018 six hurricanes and tropical storms appeared on radars at once.

We now have 'rain bombs'. In 2017 Hurricane Harvey dropped a million gallons of water for every single person in the entire state of Texas, killing sixty-eight and causing a hundred and twenty-five billion dollars' worth of damage (but they still voted for Trump who called climate change a Chinese hoax to ruin American business).

Suhayla, a journalist, was the last person I met while making this show. She told me her story.

Suhayla (*voice-over*) Bangladesh is at the epicentre of the global climate crisis. Eighty per cent of the country is floodplain and is affected by floods, storms, riverbank erosions, cyclones and droughts. Unless greenhouse gas emissions are controlled now, the situation will become unmanageable.

After speaking along with the recording, the actor speaks directly as Suhayla.

Suhayla My family is from a village in Bangladesh called Kara Mura
    As kids we loved visiting, my brother and me exploring the rice paddies, seeing the farm hands tend the cows, fishing in one of the small lakes or fushkunis, watching my grandmother, Rani, cook one of her famous fish curries.
    As a teenager Ma would bring out the photos and I would wriggle with boredom. Pay attention, Suhayla, she would say, these are your roots. Who cares? I thought. I had important stuff to do, like meeting my friends for the new Spice Girls movie. But I still called my grandmother every fortnight.

The last time we went on holiday to our family bari the road stopped suddenly half a mile away from the village, it

13

was completely flooded. We boarded a small bamboo boat, a nowka, and then meandered down the murky green water for three hours.

Slowly my parents stopped planning to go home to retire

In Kara Mura the rain was coming at times when it is not supposed to and not coming when it should. The world of their parents, drowning. The last visit they made, they had tried to persuade my grandparents Rani and Ram to come to the UK. The idea appalled them. Leave their home? Your home is leaving you, my father had said. Then we got the news that my grandfather and uncle had drowned in a sudden flash flood, leaving only my grandmother. We were distraught. I told my parents I had to go see Dadi-ma.

So I am thirty thousand feet in the air. Heading to the place Mum and Dad called home.

CAPTION: *Earth*.

Aaron (*voice-over*) So you're watching landscapes which are changing in the space of a generation, you know, like they've not changed for thousands and thousands of years. It's disturbing.

I spent quite a bit of time talking to the First Nations people in the Arctic, they were in a state of disbelief and quite a lot of trauma at the loss of their heritage, their way of life

The understanding of who they were in the landscape

Not being able to go fishing and hunting in ways that they used to.

April Their connection to the landscape being torn from them?

Aaron (*voice-over*) There are these dwarf trees – they can't grow very high because it's so cold – they grow on the permafrost which is only few inches below the surface of the soil which is only really a mat of mosses that the roots are growing through – and now as the permafrost is thawing the trees start falling over but they keep trying to grow towards the light and so you get these wonky trees that are all wobbly and we call them drunken forests because everything is kind of crossing and wobbling everywhere and the ground is all lumpy and bumpy so trying to get across from A to B is like walking through an *Alice in Wonderland* landscape, you're having to zigzag all over the place and you have a sense of it being really eerie, disturbing when you think what it's telling you. Because everything is connected and therefore we should be cautious in how we treat the world – that's something I feel very strongly, this is such a hugely complicated Earth system, that we are dependent on for everything, yet we are going round like a bull in china shop and I think that's terrifying in terms of how we are destroying what we don't yet understand, yet rely on totally.

April Soil is disappearing. Seventy-five billion tons lost each year due to intensive farming practices and excess rainfall. Soil erosion in the UK is currently at unsustainable levels.

More carbon dioxide in the air produces nutritional declines across the board – drops in protein content as well as in iron, zinc and B vitamins
    Since 1950 much of the good stuff in the plants we grow – protein, calcium, iron, vitamin C – has declined by as much as one-third. Everything is becoming more like junk food – even the protein content of bee pollen has dropped by a third.
    The great nutrient collapse – CO_2 makes plants bigger but dilutes nutrients in the food supply.

Climate change means an empire of hunger.

At two-point-five degrees the ensuing drought would mean the world needed more calories than it could produce. But anthropogenic climate change is already a reality in Africa.

In East Africa, 2011 saw the worst drought in sixty years, in East Africa eighty-two per cent of glaciers on Kilimanjaro have vanished and rivers are drying up. In

Nigeria half the population has no access to water. Catastrophic flooding in North Africa and Mozambique left one million people hungry. Droughts, heat stress and flooding have led to a reduction in food productivity in a continent that was already under pressure. With rainfall below average in Ethiopia, Kenya and Somalia, East Africa faces the worst food crisis in the twenty-first century.

These facts I'm bringing you. They're harbingers. They show us what we will be facing sooner than we like to think. It's hard to believe that our reality, the here and now, could be any different, but to save ourselves we have to begin to try and imagine it.

2. EARTH FUTURE NIGHTMARE

April It's a miracle we had slept through it
    I wake up to my husband shouting up the stairs,
    We're fucking flooded.
    I grab a jumper and some jeans.
    Downstairs a stinking, brown metre of water covers the living room
    And it's still raining
    It has been raining for weeks
    Looking out of the window the same fetid brown water is barrelling along the street
    I reached for my phone
    Every headline. The Thames Barrier has failed. I think of our next-door neighbour and her paved garden. No chance of the soil absorbing the rainwater there. Times that by millions is part of the problem. Bit unfair to blame her for catastrophic global heating but she is handy.

There is no point trying to rescue any of the downstairs possessions – they will be rife with bacteria and need burning.
    I feel an overwhelming need to cry. This is my home, my stuff. I try to phone my son. He is living in Rotherhithe, it's

low-lying so the rent's cheaper – No answer. A kick of fear in the pit of my stomach.

What can we do but wait it out upstairs – wait for the water to recede? Last time people had died, panicking and fleeing their homes. The metre-deep water was deceptively fast-flowing and losing your balance could be fatal. Stay put was the advice. If that becomes impossible seek higher ground. Last time the water had begun to recede after five days, leaving a toxic sludge over everything. We had got sick – stomach cramps, diarrhoea – just to add to the general nightmare, but we were lucky, our kids were grown up. How parents of young kids managed was beyond me. Mothers shouting Don't touch it – hold my hand – stay upstairs! Little lost faces at windows. No water – sewage had contaminated the reservoirs. We had rescued tins from the kitchen and eaten stuff out of them cold.

Thousands of acres of good arable land had been flooded
Potatoes rotted in the ground, cabbages, carrots, lettuce. There had been a massive fresh vegetable shortage that year.

Awful pictures of those caught on the tube as the water submerged the underground system. People had recorded it on their mobile phones.

I feel a different kind of water rise up in my mind – a dark emotion flooding me –

How could I live like this? I curl up in a ball on my bed – the nightmare is happening again.

I ring my son – his phone is dead. It couldn't mean anything, could it? I had forgotten the stench of floodwater – filled with run-off from factory farms, hazardous chemical waste, sewage and soil. It floats up choking me. Husband comes into the room. The rain's not stopping they say and another storm's on the way. I pull the covers over my head. I don't want to believe it. I want to scream and shout but that frankly would be pathetic. I think we should go now, he says, while we have the chance.

Lights change.

There are a hell of a lot of cows on this planet
   Sixty per cent of mammals are livestock, pigs and cows
   Thirty-six per cent humans
   Just four per cent of mammals are wild
   In Brazil and Australia there are more cows than people
   It takes eight pounds of grain to create one hamburger
   Plus six hundred and sixty gallons of water
   Add the methane farts of cows adding to the greenhouse
effect.

It takes six-point-six-one pounds of CO_2 to produce a
pound of beef
   And only zero-point-zero-three to produce a pound of
potatoes.

In 2018 Jair Bolsonaro was elected president of Brazil
promising to open the Amazon forest to development,
which is to say deforestation for cattle farming.

Deforestation fires have reduced the Amazon by thirty per
cent. A feedback loop. Forest fires release carbon dioxide so
the planet heats up, causing more, bigger fires that consume
more of the forest, and soon we are left with not the biggest
carbon sink but a producer of carbon, the magnificent
rainforest transmogrified to dry savannah.

The wildfires threaten the three hundred thousand
indigenous people who live in the forest. They see
themselves as guardians of that land for all of us. In 2020 a
hundred and ten indigenous activists were murdered.

Eighty per cent of Amazon deforestation is for livestock.

Suhayla It's a bit of a kick in the guts when I arrive – this
time the journey by boat is two hours longer to reach the
village – what's left of it – isolated baris scattered along the
soggy land – people travel by boat now to visit each other. I
call to mind the lush green-gold stretches of rice fields now
vanished. I reach our bari – water lapping at the gate of the
farm. Dadi-ma comes to meet me and takes my face in her

hands and gives me a blessing. She looks smaller than before and her hair is completely white. She still won't let me do anything, she tells me she's going to make me make my favourite dish. I insist on helping her prepare the meal, she grumbles at me but we slice the fish. Coriander, red onion chopped, garlic and chillis crushed, my grandmother's hands are very quick but I notice a slight shake. On top of the fish she throws the spices then heats the oil, the fish sizzles immediately. The smell is delicious. She picks at her food – she can't eat much now, she says. I musn't worry about her. She tells me that Abani, my cousin's wife, is here with her small daughter, Anya. Abani appears, smiles, she is elegant with a long thick plait of hair. She takes over, shows me my room, watches while I fumble with my mosquito net – she steps in and efficiently sets it up, she tells me because of all the water they are more vicious now. Anya hangs behind but then grows more confident. Three years old, curious, with big bright eyes and fingers into everything. They both help me unpack. Abani and Anya were a double act, I discovered – Anya found the portable charger for my laptop battery and held it up and said, What is it? Abani said, Don't ask so many questions! Anya looked at me, big dark eyes then pointed to my camera, What is it? Now it was a great game. It's my camera, I told her – I'm a journalist. I want to record Kara Mura. Maybe I'll take pictures of you.

Abani says, Will you record my story? Then you can tell people what is happening to us.

Abani – the name means 'Earth'.

That night Rani had gone to bed and Anya was asleep, she came and sat at the end of my bed. We talked till it got light. She married Gopal my cousin four years ago. Anya was born a year later. She asks me if I have children. When I tell her no, she asks me what does my mother say? I say, She says there must be a person crazy enough to take me on somewhere. Abani laughs.

Once she had taught at the primary school in her village. She used to teach the children a Tagore poem.

After speaking along with the recording, the actor speaks directly as Abani.

Abani (*voice-over*) And when old words die out on the tongue
New melodies break forth from the heart
And where the old tracks are lost
New country is revealed with its wonders.

Suhayla Tell me what happened?

Abani At eight o'clock one night, when Anya was just a few months old, the rain began to beat on the corrugated tin of the roof, like hammers. A powerful wind started up, shaking the shutters and doors. We looked out and saw the trees over the road being pushed horizontal by its force. Then with a sickening, grating rip the roof of our neighbours' house was peeled off and tossed away. This storm was different from the storms we had known in the past. We sat in the darkness – then suddenly a mass of water smashed in through the door and Gopal's father shouted that the river had broken its banks. I held Anya close, tiny, fragile, and we fled, running for higher ground in the driving rain and screeching wind. We huddled together with some of our neighbours and watched the river, a swollen monster, black, swift-moving, swallowing everything, houses dragged into its path and destroyed. I prayed what warmth was left in my body would keep Anya warm. The next days the river retreated leaving a blanket of mud where our house had been, the wind had ripped out my father-in-law's fruit trees, carried off rice and tea from the family's small shop and crumbled the mud walls of the house as if a giant had crushed it in its fists. Huge waves at sea had pushed salt water into the river and so the fish in our pond, dead from salt water. The sea is torturing us, Rani said. Huge chunks of land at the edges of the river broke off and the soil was washed away. Your parents sent money and we rebuilt the bari on brick plinths to protect us from floods. Now though we had less to eat. We suffered from skin rashes and pains in our stomach from the salty water, and the village struggled to grow its rice crop and vegetables. We diversified into shrimp farming but it was difficult because harvesting the shrimps gave us very little money. The food we did grow was not like before. I was pregnant again and very sick. I had pains in my stomach, headaches and dizziness. The clinic told us it was the water, it was dangerous for pregnant women. They gave me aspirin and wished me luck. I lost the baby.

Suhayla The light was coming through the chinks in the shutters when we finished talking. I hugged Abani and she went back to her room. I heard Rani call to me. I went into her room and got into bed on my grandfather's side. We held hands and she drifted off to sleep. I lay awake thinking of what Abani had told me.

CAPTION: *Fire.*

April The world is on fire from the Amazon to California, from Australia to the Siberian Arctic.
  Do we watch the world burn or do we choose to do what is necessary to achieve a different future?

During the 2019 to 2020 Australian bushfire season, strong winds and extreme heat drove wildfires.
  The old ways of fighting these fires are increasingly redundant
  Australian firefighters said they were frightened
  The idea that a fire could generate a tornado as it did in Australia in 2003 seemed hard for scientists to credit but many more fire tornadoes have occurred since then. Thunderstorms created by the intense energy of the fire can shoot out lightning that ignites fires twenty miles ahead of the fire's front line. They are known as Pyro-Cbs. Australia generated eighteen of them last year.

Forty-six million acres were burnt, thirty-four people died, as well as three billion terrestrial vertebrates including thirty thousand koalas. One hundred and three billion dollars in economic losses. NASA estimates that three hundred and six million tons of carbon dioxide were released into the atmosphere.

Feedback loops.

As Greta Thunberg says, Our house is on fire. Why aren't we doing something about it?

Because we have too much faith in human progress?
 Because it's not happening to us – not yet anyway?
 Because we are so sociopathically good at collating bad news into a sickening sense of what constitutes 'normal'?

Aaron (*voice-over*) I had one particular meeting with a fireman
 He had just spent the whole summer travelling all over the north of the boreal forest trying to put out these wildfires with his team
 Fires are part of the landscape but they're not supposed to be that common, that fierce
 The biggest city is Yellow Knife and they almost had to be evacuated
 Forty thousand people were told to stay in their houses for a week because of wildfires
 And the air pollution was so horrendous you couldn't breathe
 And the other thing was the water levels in the lakes were so low
 because of the drought
 And the heatwaves, that they couldn't power the city's hydroelectric dam
 So they had to set up a system of generators and have a diesel convoy
 Endlessly coming from miles away.

Ironic – having to turn to the most polluting fuel in the world which is actually driving the climate crisis.

April We're talking about fire but also air and water.

Aaron (*voice-over*) Like I said.

April Connected, yes.

CAPTION: *Water.*

Rising ocean waters are possibly the biggest threat we face and will completely inundate many coastal land areas in the next three decades.

Places that will be underwater by 2050 include:

PROJECTION: *The Bahamas, Bruges, London. Bangkok, Panama City, Ho Chi Minh City, the Adriatic coast, Alexandria, Mumbai, Shanghai, Manila, Mozambique, Florida Keys, Charleston, San Francisco Bay, New Orleans, New York City and this theatre.*

By the middle of the century the ocean may contain more plastic by weight than fish.

Every year we plough an undersea area twice the size of the United States with trawlers levelling everything on the seafloor.

The overfishing and the dead zones at the mouths of all major rivers where fertilisers pour into the sea, and the gyres of plastic spinning slowly a thousand miles offshore, these are the smallest of our insults to the ocean.

The overwhelming threat comes from burning fossil fuels

Ninety-three per cent of extra heat is actually collecting in the sea

The deep sea is now warming nine times faster than in the 1980s.

Half the coral reefs, once vibrant with colour are now a shade of murk

The volumes of carbon we are producing – it turns out even the ocean is too small to soak up without effect

It turns the sea water into carbonic acid

The oceans have seen their acidity increase by thirty per cent

Increasing ocean acidification, heating and deoxygenation mean our oceans are heading for a tipping point – a qualitative change in a system from which recovery to the initial system is impossible.

Kay (*voice-over*) Anything beyond two degrees we're tipping into tipping points where we could escalate into the four-degree mark and the five-degree mark and it would just go on and on

And society doesn't know if it could survive

And no one's done the work to find out if we can survive

And I doubt it.

April By 2050 all the coral reefs will be dead.

Fish and shellfish will be unable to make their skeletons, their shells

By the end of the century the oceans will be hot, sour and breathless.

One in three people have no access to safe drinking water.

As the glaciers melt the UN predicts a massive increase in water scarcity –

Two billion people will be without fresh water.

England could suffer major water shortages by 2030 due to increasing droughts due to climate change.

London is one of the eleven cities most likely to run out of drinking water.

CAPTION: *The Future.*

To turn on a tap and have nothing come out. The reassuring gush; water, quenched thirst, cleanliness, health. The flow of normal life. Stopped. Ominous. Something big somewhere gone wrong. I remember hearing in 2015 that Cape Town had reached Day Zero and the implementation of level-seven water restrictions. But Cape Town was away. Another continent. It couldn't happen here, could it?

2030 and I'm waiting again. A different queue. Hundreds of us with plastic containers, bottles. The lorry is late. I am about fifty yards back on the line. It's hard to keep positive. To get out of bed to make the front of the queue. I have not brushed my teeth and my mouth feels gummy. The woman behind me has a kid who is crying, thirsty. I try to be nice. It's hard when you haven't had a shower or a cup of tea. When you know you smell. We had been saving rainwater at home for washing our bits but the last week it's been bone dry. Swimming pools are unheard of in level eight.

The woman smiles back nervously at me. I look into her eyes. There are two expressions you see nowadays – numbness or panic. She holds hard to the hand of her toddler. Still no lorry. People are grumbling. Suddenly there is a woman moving towards us from further back in the line – she points her finger accusingly at the woman behind me – You're not from here – you don't live here. She's from Hoe Street! Let's see your ration card. The woman tells them they've made a mistake. Her bag is grabbed before there is anything she can do – her child is whimpering and clinging to its mummy – who is pushed to the ground. I told you, Hoe Street, says the woman triumphantly. My neighbour, Trudi, who is seventy and lovely, says, Does it matter? And helps the woman up. Trudi is a church-goer. She says, If your enemy is hungry give him food to eat and if he is thirsty give him water to drink. I was late this morning and the lorry was only half full, says the young mother. They told me to come here. Fuck off, says her assailant. And then to Trudi, And you can fuck off too, you communist. Then we see our lorry with its tank of water trundle towards us. The woman and child walk reluctantly away. I'd like to say, Stop I'll share – but something stops me. The memory of thirst.

As the queue surges forward, Trudi is pushed aside. I'm ashamed to say I pretend not to notice and push forward too. Those at the back always walk away empty-handed.

Suhayla It was a real moment for me going back and being with my grandma and hearing this story and realising that wasn't the weather anymore – this was different, this was frightening. And I understood why Abani wanted me to tell this story.

Abani Then this year we suffered another storm – they give them names – this one was called Cyclone Mora, which is frustrating – because it gives the impression you can talk to them and say, Come on, Mora, you don't want to do that really, do you? But she wasn't listening.

We ran again. I grabbed Anya, now a toddler, and begged Gopal to leave the animals and come to higher ground but this time your grandfather and uncle went out into the darkness and tried to rescue their remaining cows, the poor animals drowning in the river. Again the water took everything. Our house went into the water but this time also the land it had stood on that was our shrimp farm. The wind picked up anything, helpless and tossed it like a doll. The water seemed to want to obliterate the land, like a dark force. Your grandfather and uncle did not come back. We found their bodies three miles upriver. Grief. Rani was inconsolable. I tried to explain to Anya what had happened but three is too young to understand. Everyday she asks me where are Babu and Uncle – are they coming back today? Not today, I answer.

Aaron (*voice-over*) Climate denial campaigns have been very, very effective in delaying action – undermining the good science that had been done

The system is corrupted by vested interests, fossil fuel companies for example, who are not good faith actors to society

It has strong connections to tobacco campaigns

Some of same people – same PR industries

America had just gone through the winning of the Cold War and they needed a new enemy. Environmentalism seemed like a threat to the free market worldview cos it required government regulation of big business – fossil fuel companies made the most of that because they gave money to institutes so these people got in front of the cameras.

April I heard a story about a scientist who was asked to talk to some major business leaders.

They paid her a years' wages to come to talk to them
She told them the kind of stuff I've been telling you
And at the end of it they said, Well where is the best place for us to go to get away from it?

She said, No, you don't understand, there is no away
Come on, they said, is this place New Zealand or Alaska?
She said again, There is no away

Then they said, Okay – I will build myself a bunker but I have a problem, how do I ensure that my security guards don't kill me and take the code to open my food supplies?

Where are we on AI? Could I employ robots? Or is there some kind of collar I could get my security to wear that will inflict pain if they disobey me?

I don't know what she said but I hope it was Fuck you.

CAPTION: 2030.

It was the day the food distribution depots didn't open. The rusty shutters stayed down bearing a sign: *Please halve your daily rations till further notice.* And that was it. The news is blaming immigrants for getting through the militarised border and using counterfeit ration cards.

At some point that afternoon in the fitful sleep hunger brings I am woken by shouts. I move to the window. The self-appointed patriots' patrol is circling a woman who is talking back to them, her face anguished. Speak English, they bark at her. She carries her child on her back, its thin face, turned like a half-moon, lies silent on her shoulder blade. She turns to the patrol to show the child, suddenly a shot rings out and the woman is on the ground. I run out of the house propelled by an energy I haven't felt in months shouting, No, no.

Another shot.

One of the men turns to me and tells me to get back indoors. I can't move.

Where's Trudi? I need her – and then I remember she had died too. A tick bite. The nasty things had a firm hold in the biosphere due to increased temperatures and it had finished her.

In the road lay the woman and child unmoving and bloody.

They are the first dead bodies I had ever seen and it pours out, all my anger, disbelief, horror.

God knows who is listening but I am past the point of caring and I'm saying things I shouldn't –

Later my doorbell rings. Two men. They show their official status with a flash of their phones. I've heard about this and now it's here at my door. The men, government officials, tell me I have been overheard criticising the government's handling of the ecological emergency. People can have their ration cards removed for six weeks for such infringements. My husband comes downstairs, anxious, he's coughing – a cough that never seems to have an end.

I say that whoever reported me must be mistaken. I don't talk like that. That's not the sort of person I am. Just like everyone else I want my rations. I want food in my belly. A human is nothing without it, and then I look at my husband, who is giving me our 'shut up' signal. It's like I am sounding too radical with my talk of human beings.

I smile and offer them a cup of tea. It's worth the sacrifice of our last teabags to sweeten them up. I make the tea in our kitchen, boiling the water on our one-ring gas appliance. But then there is a flicker and suddenly the power is off. We are plunged into darkness. I search for the candle – why do I never leave it in the same place? I grope my way to the front room. The men have left, taking our ration books pending further investigation. I stand there in the cold, hungry, with the small flickering flame of the candle in front of my husband who is probably dying. It's game over, the thought comes swiftly as a sudden draught guts my candle.

Abani This time our land was washed away, our shrimp farm gone, there is no life for us here anymore.

The land cannot not sustain us.

We have Anya and no choice but to try to find work in Dhaka. Gopal has gone ahead already and we will join him. When I told Anya we were leaving this place we know in every light, every season, she said she would take a photograph with her memory and she blinked her eyes twice like a lizard.

I still cannot cry. I am too numb. Too shocked, too scared. I'm like one of our fruit trees – ripped from the earth by the pitiless water – and now lying frozen – roots bared – sticking out like dead fingers into emptiness. I don't want to go to Dhaka

To live in a room in a Kamrangirchar built over an old rubbish dump for twenty pounds a week. I don't want to work in the garment trade. I don't want to think of Gopal in the brick works. What if Anya gets sick? I am so anxious for her. The air is gritty from traffic fumes and the smoke of cooking fires. The Buriganga river is thick with the slick of chemicals from factories. You cannot wash in it.

There must be another life for us? Ours has been stolen from us.

Suhayla I try to talk to my grandma about her future.

She says, I know what you are up to, child. If you think I will leave the land where I was born, where I have buried my husband and son, you can think again. And she marches off to feed her chickens.

I sit down on the porch to finish transcribing Abani's story, the light glowing on my laptop. I feel helpless. Abani and Anya are packing for their journey to Dakha, but I know that Rani won't ever leave here.

As I write, the first drops of rain begin to fall.

For Bangladesh the one-point-five degrees of warming we have already signed up to will mean more flooding, landslides, poverty, temperature rises and displacement.

A storm was building.

I go to my grandmother. I point to the sky – at the roiling clouds – It's a storm, I say. It's not safe here. The neighbours are good, she says, we help each other. Where else will I get such good neighbours? And that is the last word she will say on the matter. I anxiously watch the sky, the rain is endless. Some people leave on boats while they can, but my grandmother refuses.

The water rises so fast.
    A force that could not be commanded. Enraged nature. Abani holds Anya while I help Dadi-ma. Inside there is just darkness, no lights. We are suddenly pushed off our feet by a force of water and Anya is knocked from Abani's arms. She screams her name – I scream into the darkness too, and Abani flings herself after her daughter. Dadi-ma goes limp in my arms. Let me go too, she whispers, let me go. And my heart breaks. I wish myself back to a year, two years, five, a decade. To when there was still time to save them.

Later in London I finished writing Abani's story. I promised her I'd tell it, so I am.

April If the seven-point-five billion people on the planet had the carbon footprint of a person living in Bangladesh we would require an Earth the size of Asia to live sustainably. Our planet would be far more than enough for us. If everyone on Earth had the carbon footprint of a person living in China, the planet Earth would be enough.
    But if we all had the carbon footprint of a citizen of the UK, we would need two-and-a-half planet Earths. In the US, four Earths.

I've tried to give you the science.
    Stayed stoic – on the whole – while doing it.

Here we are part of a system that is extractive, wasteful, linear, abusive

That takes from the Earth with no heed of the consequences for people like Suhayla and her family

How can we look into the faces of children and tell them what we are doing?

When our media won't tell us the truth, when our politicians pretend they are taking it seriously but lie.

But what if all they think about is the market and their shares in the companies that are profiting from the trashing of our planet?

Why are we letting such a tiny group of people trash our planet for their greed?

And when will the tipping points come that will rock the Earth into a death spiral?

Why aren't we acting like it's an emergency?

Like it's World War Two?

Because this is bigger. This is a thousand holocausts.

And the thing is, we have the solutions. We have them now.

But we also have this.

She picks up a bucket of oil.

Our government says it wants to take action on climate change but subsidises the oil industry giants to the tune of ten and a half billion pounds a year.

The world's top sixty banks have spent three-point-eight trillion dollars financing the fossil fuel industry since the Paris agreement in 2015.

If we want to know why things aren't changing, it's because some people are making a huge amount of money – from this.

April pours the oil over the stage as in a spill. She is affected physically by the oil on her body. She may 'drink' the oil as oil-slick rebels do – impersonating the act of drinking oil.

Chidi (*voice-over*) Shell had arrived in Nigeria in the 1950s and were drilling in a largely under-regulated way

Millions of people, animals, local flora, have been displaced and destroyed by negligence and greed

The life expectancy of environmentalists is very very short. One of more famous story is of Ken Saro-Wiwa executed by firing squad by the Nigerian government.

That execution was based on pressure and financial influence of Big Oil in the region but he is only one of a very big number of people who have simply disappeared

Big Oil dictates the standards of human rights in certain places.

Shell wouldn't be allowed to rock up to a small Scottish village

Mow down the mayor

And indefinitely pollute the land and waters in the surrounding areas indefinitely

But they do that in the Niger Delta.

Aaron (*voice-over*) I've had a dark night of the soul.

I constantly have a sense of grief and loss for what we are losing

I was a zoologist, that was my initial passion for the planet and the amazing diversity of life and the sense that already half the Great Barrier Reef has died and every report that comes out, more birds on the verge of extinction, more insect population loss, we're losing the magic of the world, it's heartbreaking

I'm grief-stricken, heartbroken

Full of rage against the stupidity of it all.

Elise (*voice-over*) I can't sit back and look at their lovely little kiddie faces and not do anything about it

I remember thinking they're going to be really proud of their aunty

And one day when they're older and they ask me what did you do?

Cos when everything – hopefully not – not trying to be negative, but when things have turned to shit
And they say you were around at that time, what were you doing?
That they know I tried in whatever way I could.
Things were like this and now they're like this.
I don't know.

Xanthe (*voice-over*) The actual future, I think it's going to be very different
And what people are learning in, like, everyday normal school isn't really gonna help
I think the skills I'm currently learning, like, living in a community will actually be very useful.

Chidi (*voice-over*) We need to move forward to a vision of a better society, our young people need to have a vision of a world they want to see and not be fearful of the world they are in.

CAPTION: *The UK will host the next COP talks in Glasgow 2021.*
It remains to be seen whether governments will take the necessary steps to avoid the continuance of the breakdown of our global climate and ecological systems. Environmentalists are calling these talks 'our' last chance.

Chidi (*voice-over*) It's so important to find a group you want to work with – you'll find a groundswell of incredible people out there who want to create things you can build on.
Even though you are told by newspapers that are owned by billionaires that you can't fight billionaires, you just might find you win.

Aaron (*voice-over*) Radical change
Happens very quickly
There are a lot of signs that the system is close to its social tipping points in many ways

The fossil fuel industries teetering
Renewable energy is becoming a viable alternative
And if that's amplified by policy and movements
You could start to see the existing system crumbling very quickly
We need more people putting pressure wherever they can
Each of us has a specialism to contribute – how does it intersect with the struggle?
How do I mobilise my community to put more pressure on?
We have to keep fighting because we don't know how close we are to fundamentally shifting things.
As Nelson Mandela is famous for saying, when he was finally released from Robben Island, It always seemed impossible till it was done.

Chidi (*voice-over*) I would urge everyone buy fair trade – that impact on poorer farmers further down the line is huge
Get a green electricity company
Use a paper bag, a cloth bag
Don't bank with a bank that is bankrolling this kind of industry, effectively using your money to fund things that are in your detriment.
Close your account at Barclays
Move your money to an ethical bank
After that go out and find a group of like-minded people
Find your tribe
Join your local XR, your local environmental group
Do fun things that that raise awareness
Things that are enjoyable because of the camaraderie.
Unfurl and develop that personal sense of mission.

Helen (*voice-over*) You have to
Get through the denial to the grief
There was a powerful moment
With my son
We were walking down Southwark Bridge, no idea what would happen

And that moment when we stepped off the pavement
onto the road
    When we took the bridge with all those others
    That for me was the start
    Actually the road doesn't belong to anybody
    We stepped over something
    This whole business of obeying
    How we have been coerced into something
    Subliminally coerced.

Something that had seemed so hard
    Was so simple
    Powerful.

April Every story has a multitude of possible endings. And
there are always strong clues to where a story is headed.
Warning signs. Moments when characters, groups,
governments, nations, can make choices that will change
everything. And our lives are going to change.
    The choice is whether we are going to be in control of
that change
    Or it's going to happen to us in the most terrifying way.

Bangladesh is at the forefront of climate adaptation and
they've built twelve thousand functioning cyclone shelters,
an early warning system, and they've engaged people at a
local grassroots and national level. Which has saved
millions of lives. They listened to the warning signs. And
they did something about it. They managed to change their
story.

And as Suhayla promised to tell Abani's story, I promised
to tell Suhayla's.

Suhayla The water was rising so fast, we knew if we stayed
we would be lost. We struggled through the raging waters, I
held Rani, Abani and Anya, and we managed at last to get
pulled into a neighbours' boat which took us to the nearest
shelter. It was terrifying. But we all survived.

April In 2020 a quarter of the country was flooded, over a million homes damaged, hundreds and thousands of people marooned. Super-Cyclone Amphan was called the storm of the century.

Kara Mura was washed away. They survived, but there was nowhere for Rani to return to. Because no matter how prepared they are in Bangladesh, if rich countries don't stop emitting, then by 2030 one billion people will be displaced by man-made climate change.

So I have brought you back – not to where we were when we started out – not to safety – but how safe was that place?

Two-point-six degrees Celsius of warming is worse than two-point-three degrees, which is worse than two-point-one.

We have to fight for every fraction of every degree. Not just for ourselves but for climate justice.

Abani And when old words die out on the tongue
    New melodies break forth from the heart
    And where the old tracks are lost
    New country is revealed with its wonders.

April I said I wouldn't get emotional but maybe that's wrong. Maybe we should be emotional. Full of rage at what's being done to us and our fellow humans and the Earth and all future life? Maybe emotional is exactly just what we should be.

Climate change is the greatest crisis humankind has ever faced and unless we address it together we will face it alone.